D0606422

Fact Finders®

ANATOMY CLASS

Human Muscles

by Jodi Wheeler-Toppen, PhD

Consultant:
Marjorie J. Hogan, MD
Associate Professor
University of Minnesota, Minneapolis

WITHDRAWN

Capstone press®

Mankato, Minnesota

Fact Finders is published by Capstone Press,
151 Good Counsel Drive, P.O. Box 669, Mankato, Minnesota 56002.
www.capstonepress.com

Books published by Capstone Press are manufactured with paper
containing at least 10 percent post-consumer waste.

Library of Congress Cataloging-in-Publication Data
Wheeler-Toppen, Jodi.
    Human muscles / by Jodi Wheeler-Toppen.
    p. cm. — (Fact finders. Anatomy class)
    Includes bibliographical references and index.
    Summary: "Describes human muscles, including skeletal muscles and involuntary muscles, and
how they work" — Provided by publisher.
    ISBN 978-1-4296-3341-3 (library binding)
    ISBN 978-1-4296-3884-5 (softcover)
    1. Muscles — Juvenile literature. I. Title. II. Series.
QP321.W46 2010
611'.73 — dc22   2009002766

Editorial Credits
Lori Shores, editor; Ted Williams, designer; Svetlana Zhurkin, media researcher

Photo Credits
Getty Images/3D4Medical, cover, 7, 9 (inset), 10, 11; 3D Clinic, 16; Andreas Rentz, 15; Stone/David
    Madison, 26; Visuals Unlimited/Dr. Fred Hossler, 9
iStockphoto/Iris Nieves, 5; Julie Deshaies, 25 (inset)
Shutterstock/Agnieszka Steinhagen, 22; hkannn, 21; Jack Dagley Photography, 25; Sebastian
    Kaulitzki, 19; Sofia Santos, 29
Visuals Unlimited/Dr. Fred Hossler, 13; Ralph Hutchings, 13 (inset)

Essential content terms are **bold** and are defined at the bottom of the page where they first appear.

Table of Contents

Your Active Body

Imagine you are playing softball. You swing the bat and race around the bases. Home run! During all the action, you probably didn't even think about your muscles. But more than 640 muscles kicked in to make the play a success. It's a great moment for your softball team. But it was your muscle team that made it happen.

If your body were a machine, the muscles would be the engine. A car engine uses the energy in gasoline to turn the wheels. Your muscles take the energy from your lunch and use it to power all of the movements you make.

Muscles are at work even in places that might surprise you. Your heart is one giant muscle. All of your bones connect to muscles, including the tiniest bone deep in your ear. If you could peel back the layers of the human body, you'd discover a world of muscles inside.

BODY FACT

If you want to know what muscle feels like, grab some raw beef or chicken. When you eat meat, you are eating animal muscle.

Getting Under Your Skin

Imagine that you could wiggle out of your skin and look underneath. The first thing you might notice is that you are all red. Dark red muscles cover your body from head to toe.

But muscles don't just wrap around you like a blanket. Your muscles cover you in layers. They come in whatever shape it takes to get the job done. Long, thin muscles move your arms and legs. Your belly is lined with flat, rectangular muscles. The muscle that wraps around your shoulder is shaped like a triangle. And when you pucker up for a kiss, you use the round muscle that circles your mouth.

BODY FACT

Tiny muscles surround each hair in your skin. When you're cold, those muscles tighten and give you goose bumps.

More than Meets the Eye

There's more to see when you get up close with a muscle. If you look at a muscle under a microscope, you can see long, skinny cells called **muscle fibers**. Muscle fibers are easily hurt, so small groups are bundled together to make them stronger. Many bundles of muscle fibers make up one muscle.

> **muscle fiber** — a long thin cell made of many long proteins

BODY FACT

If you could put all of your muscles on a scale, they would weigh about half of your total weight.

gluteus maximus

muscle fibers

Sit on It!

When you sit down, you are perching on your gluteus maximus. It's the muscle that makes up most of your butt. The gluteus maximus connects your upper leg to the end of your backbone. It works hard when your hip needs power, like when you climb stairs. If you could lift up that large muscle and look underneath, you would find the gluteus medius. This muscle helps you walk. It's also where the doctor sticks the needle when you get a shot in the butt!

Hold on Tight

    Muscles couldn't do much work if they were flopping loose in your body. They need to be connected. Most muscles have several **tendons**. Your biggest calf muscle connects in three places. One tendon attaches to your foot. Two more tendons attach to your thighbone. The muscle in the arch of your foot has five tendons. One tendon connects to your heel bone. The other four tendons connect to your four smallest toes.

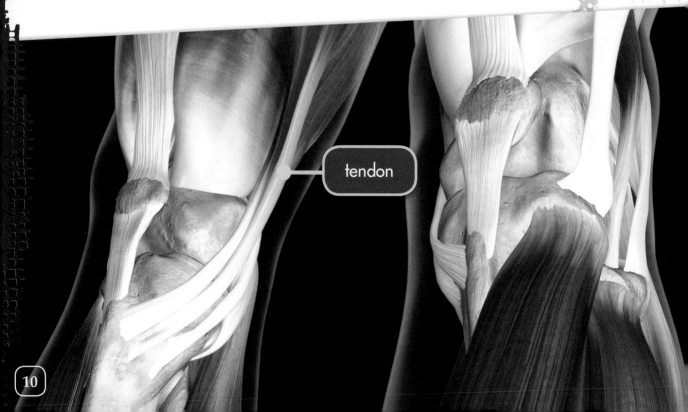

tendon

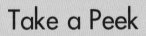

Achilles tendon
(uh-KIL-eez)

Take a Peek

Ball your hand into a fist and look at the inside of your wrist. You can see and feel your tendons through your skin. You can also feel the Achilles tendon at the back of your ankle. This tendon is named after a story about a Greek god named Achilles. According to the story, Achilles died when he was hit in the heel by an arrow. You won't die if you tear your Achilles tendon. But you will need surgery before you can walk again.

tendon — a strong band of tissue that attaches muscles to bones

CHAPTER 2

Get a Move On

Even though they come in different shapes and sizes, the muscles underneath your skin are all called skeletal muscles. These muscles attach to your skeleton, and their job is to move your bones.

Bones and muscles are shaped to work together. If you look closely at a bone, you will see hollows and grooves. These markings show where tendons were attached. Bone experts can tell how strong a person was by looking at the size of those marks. Strong muscles leave deep grooves in the bone.

BODY FACT

Some face muscles attach to skin. They help you make funny faces, like raising your eyebrows in surprise or making fish lips.

Bones develop grooves where muscles attach.

backbone

Back in Action

Your back muscles allow you to move in many directions. You can reach up for a basketball shot. You can bend forward to grab a football off the ground. You can twist sideways or lean backward to pass a note to the person behind you. Lots of muscles work together to make those movements. The spikes on your backbone make room for all of those muscles to attach.

Working Together

Skeletal muscles move the body by pulling on bones. Each muscle can get shorter, or **contract**, by itself. But a muscle can't stretch back out unless another one pulls on it. When you bend your arm, your biceps muscle contracts. This pulls your forearm up. To straighten your arm again, you use the triceps muscle located behind your arm. It pulls your forearm back down. All muscles have at least one partner that pulls in the opposite direction.

The Team Approach

Most movements require a full team of muscles. When you take a step, the muscles in your legs are on the job. But other muscles pitch in too. The muscles of your ankle, hip, belly, and back all work to help you stay upright as you walk.

---

contract — to tighten and get shorter by squeezing in toward the middle

---

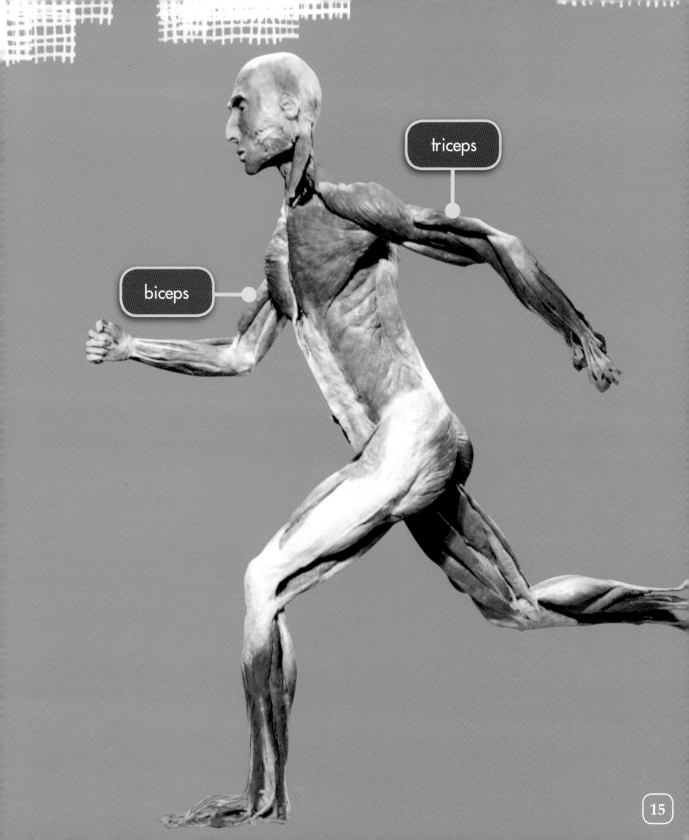

triceps

biceps

nerves

BODY FACT

On July 11, 2006, Lu Zhonghao of China lifted 201 pounds (91 kilograms) using only his little finger!

A Shrinking Solution

When you do a karate kick, muscles all over your body contract. But how do muscles actually get smaller? The action starts way down in the muscle fibers. Tiny threads of protein normally lay end to end inside muscle fibers. To contract, the threads slide together and lay side by side. When they do, the muscle fiber gets shorter and fatter.

You've Got Some Nerve

Nerves connect to muscle fibers and tell them when to contract. When you make a large movement like jumping, your nerves trigger lots of muscle fibers. When you make small, careful movements, your nerves only set a few muscle fibers in motion.

nerve — a thin fiber that sends messages between your brain and other parts of your body

CHAPTER 3

The Inside Scoop

If you could peer deep into the body, you would find more muscles hidden inside. These muscles don't connect to bones, and you can't see them move. They are the involuntary muscles that power your internal organs.

Always Working

You don't have to do much to give these muscles a workout. They are always busy. Your stomach muscles break down your food. Those same muscles help you throw up. Muscles also work hard in your intestines, lungs, and bladder.

Muscles even line your **blood vessels**. They control which parts of the body get the most blood. When you run a race, they send more blood to your legs. When you eat, they send more blood to your stomach.

blood vessel — a tube that carries blood through your body

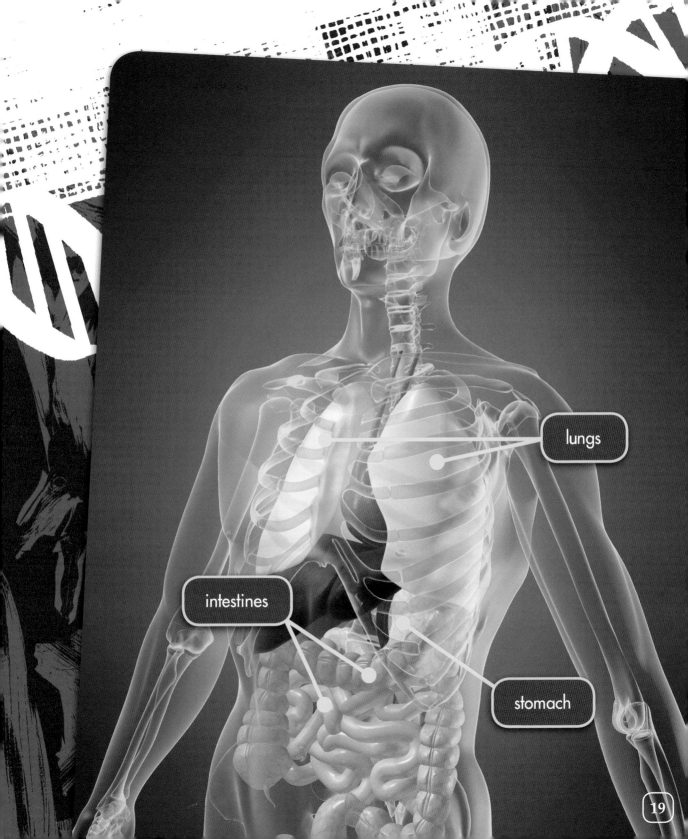

lungs

intestines

stomach

Have a Heart

Your heart is one of the strongest muscles in your body. This muscle has been beating night and day since before you were born. Your heart beats between 60 and 90 times each minute. When you exercise or get scared, it beats much faster.

Pump It Up

The heart works like a pump. First it fills up with blood. Then the muscles contract and blood gushes into the blood vessels. Each pump sends off 1/4 cup (59 mililiters) of blood. But you have about 20 cups (4.7 liters) of blood in your body. No wonder the heart has to work so hard! The muscles contract over and over to keep your blood moving.

BODY FACT

All of your blood passes through your heart once each minute. When you're doing hard exercise, it can travel through your heart in just 15 seconds.

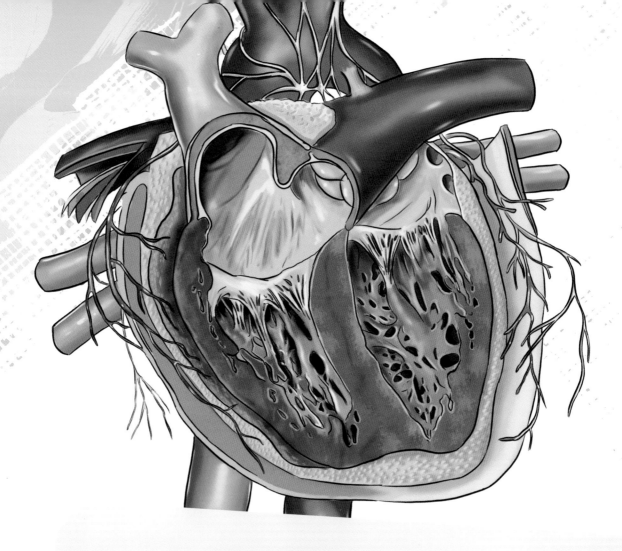

The Beat Goes On

Before the heart muscle relaxes, two valves snap shut. They keep blood from leaking backward into the heart. When the valves close, they make a "lub-dub" sound. Doctors can tell if your heart is healthy by listening to that sound through a stethoscope.

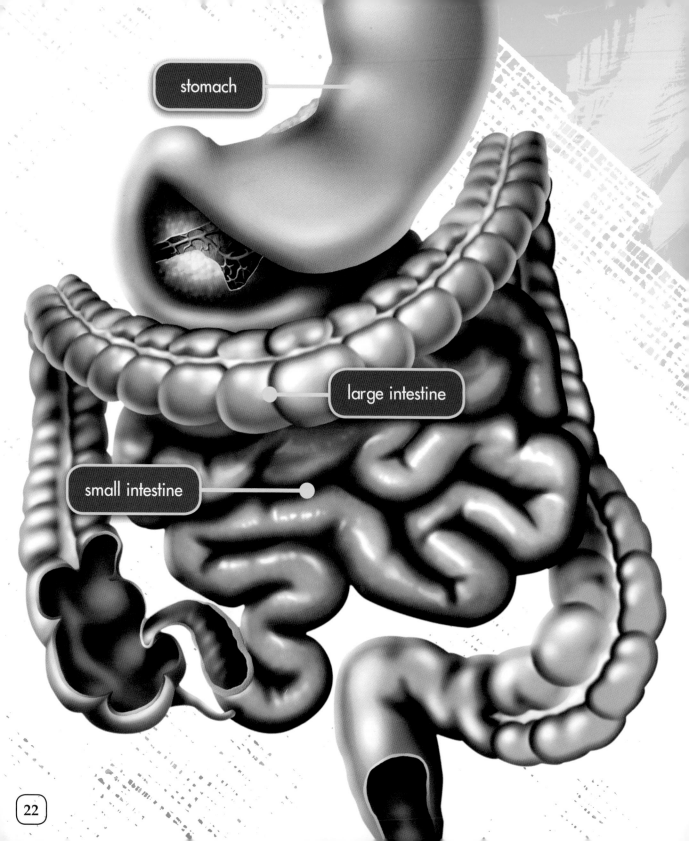

stomach

large intestine

small intestine

Moving Out

Imagine squeezing all of the toothpaste out of a tube. You would start from the bottom, and then squeeze higher and higher until you reached the top. The muscles in your digestive system work the same way. They squeeze one small section after another to move the food along. When you swallow a bite of breakfast cereal, it travels from your mouth to your stomach. Then it moves through your intestines and finally out of your body. Muscles push the food the whole way.

Hold It!

The bladder is the body's storage tank for urine. The walls of the bladder are made of involuntary muscle. These muscles can stretch to hold over 4 cups (0.9 liter) of urine. When the bladder is holding about 2 cups (0.5 liter), the muscles contract, and you feel the urge to go. But at the base of the bladder, there is a muscle you control. When you decide to relax this muscle, the pee comes out.

CHAPTER 4

Muscle Power

Remember that softball game? Playing a sport like softball helps your body get stronger. As you round the bases, your involuntary muscles send more blood to your legs. If you put your legs to work regularly, your muscle fibers will grow thicker and stronger.

Regular exercise helps all your muscles work better. Your heart gets better at pumping, and you will be able to run longer without getting tired. Exercise even helps keep the muscles in your digestive system working well.

BODY FACT

The smallest muscle in your body moves a tiny bone inside your ear. The muscle is about the size of this dash (-).

Strike a Pose

When people say, "show me your muscles," they usually want you to bend your arm. The muscle that pops out is called the biceps. An early scientist thought that bump looked like a mouse under the skin. He named it a "muscle," using the Latin word "mus" which means "little mouse." The biceps runs from just below your elbow to your shoulder. This muscle pulls up your lower arm. You can strengthen your "little mouse" by doing chin-ups.

Use It or Lose It

If you don't use your muscles, they get smaller and weaker. When you have a broken leg, the doctor puts it in a cast to keep it from moving. The cast lets the bone heal, but you can't use your leg muscles. When the cast comes off, the leg that was broken will be much thinner and weaker than your other leg. You need to exercise that leg to get it strong again.

Make Your Move

Start your engines! Your body is one powerful machine. You can jump into the air for a slam dunk. You can curl into a ball and roll down a hill. Or you can stick out your tongue and make a face at your sister. From your head to your toes, muscles keep your body on the move.

Muscles Diagram

A   **Eye** — The muscles of your eye move more than 100,000 times each day.

B   **Deltoids** — The deltoid muscles of your shoulders help you raise your arm and rotate it in all directions.

C   **Pectorals** — Without the pectoral muscles of your chest, you wouldn't be able to cross your arms.

D   **Abdominals** — Your abdominal muscles are sometimes called a "six-pack" because each muscle bulges in three places.

E   **Quadriceps** — The quadriceps femoris is actually a group of four leg muscles that stretch out your knee.

F   **Tendons** — Tendons connect muscles to bones or other muscles.

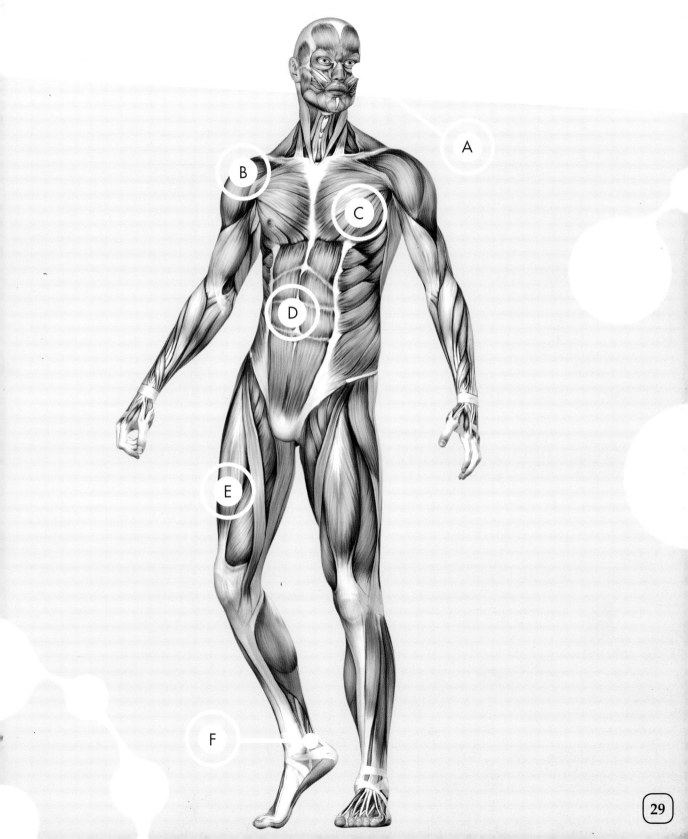

Glossary

blood vessel (BLUHD VE-suhl) — a tube that caries blood through your body; arteries and veins are blood vessels.

contract (kuhn-TRAKT) — to tighten and get shorter by squeezing in toward the middle

digestive system (dye-JESS-tiv SISS-tuhm) — the group of organs responsible for breaking down food into energy for the body and for getting rid of waste

internal (in-TUR-nuhl) — inside the body

involuntary (in-VOL-uhn-tehr-ee) — done without a person's control

muscle fiber (MUHSS-uhl FYE-bur) — a long thin cell made of many long proteins

nerve (NURV) — a thin fiber that sends messages between your brain and other parts of your body

stethoscope (STETH-uh-skope) — a medical instrument used by doctors and nurses to listen to the sounds of a patient's heart, lungs, and other areas

tendon (TEN-duhn) — a strong band of tissue that attaches a muscle to a bone

Read More

Burstein, John. *The Mighty Muscular and Skeletal Systems: How Do My Bones and Muscles Work?* Slim Goodbody's Body Buddies. New York: Crabtree, 2009.

Spilsbury, Louise. *The Skeleton and Muscles.* The Human Machine. Chicago: Heinemann, 2008.

Stewart, Gregory J. *The Skeletal and Muscular Systems.* The Human Body, How It Works. New York: Chelsea House, 2009.

Internet Sites

FactHound offers a safe, fun way to find Internet sites related to this book. All of the sites on FactHound have been researched by our staff.

Here's all you do:

Visit *www.facthound.com*

FactHound will fetch the best sites for you!

Index